WORLD WAR TWO

LIFE IN WARTIME BRITAIN

RICHARD TAMES

B. T. BATSFORD · LONDON

Typeset by Latimer Trend & Co. Ltd, Plymouth
and printed in Great Britain by BPCC Hazells Ltd,
Aylesbury

Published by B. T. Batsford Ltd 4 Fitzhardinge
Street London W1H 0AH

A catalogue record for this book is available from the British Library

ISBN 0 7134 6543 3

CONTENTS

ACKNOWLEDGMENTS

The Author and Publishers would like to thank the following for permission to reproduce illustrations: Peter Newark's Historical Pictures for pages 9, 24, 36, 49; E. T. Archive for page 8; Magnum Photos Ltd for pages 11, 14, 21, 30, 35, 38, 43, 48, 52, 57; Topham Picture Library for pages 15, 16, 18, 28, 44, 46, 55; The Hulton-Deutsch Collection for pages 13, 22, 26, 32, 41, 53, 56, 59, 60; and the Imperial Tobacco Co. for page 7. Thanks also to Mr Dave Davis for the map on page 31.

The cover illustrations show damage done by a V-2 rocket to Farringdon Street Market in London, which struck at a busy time killing 380 people (courtesy Hulton-Deutsch Collection); and, in colour, a Government poster encouraging women to work in factories during the war (courtesy Peter Newark's Historical Pictures).

USEFUL TERMS

AA — Anti-Aircraft (also known as ack-ack)

ABCA — Army Bureau of Current Affairs (organized discussions for troops)

AFS — Auxiliary Fire Service

ARP — Air Raid Precautions

ATS — Auxiliary Territorial Services (the women's army)

BEF — British Expeditionary Force (troops in France 1939–40)

CO — conscientous objector (someone who refuses to support war on grounds of principle)

ENSA — Entertainments National Service Association (organized shows and concerts in camps and factories: nicknamed Every Night Something Awful)

EWO — Essential Work Order (regulation which prevented people in key jobs being sacked or resigning)

GI — Government Issue (mark stamped on US War Department kit; hence name for a US serviceman)

LDV — Local Defence Volunteers (later the Home Guard)

POW — Prisoner of War

RAF — Royal Air Force

WAAF — Women's Auxiliary Air Force

WRNS — Women's Royal Naval Service

WVS — Women's Voluntary Service

DON'T YOU KNOW THERE'S A WAR ON?

IN THE SHADOW OF THE GREAT WAR

When the 'Great War' broke out in August 1914 people in Britain had enjoyed a century of peace almost unbroken since the Battle of Waterloo in 1815. Most of the country's wars had been colonial campaigns, fought in far-off corners of the empire. Even the war of 1854–6 against Russia, another European power, had been fought on the shores of the Black Sea, at the other end of the continent.

In 1914 very few British people, even in government and military circles, had any idea that they had committed themselves to a war that would involve fighting from China to the Falkland Islands; one that would end only when Germany had nothing left to fight with and the United States would suddenly emerge as the mighty make-weight on the Allied side.

> *United Kingdom Manpower Losses 1914–18*
> **Dead 812,317**
> **Wounded 1,849,494**

Most people expected that there would be one huge, decisive battle and that the war would be 'over by Christmas' – what happened was a series of huge, indecisive battles. Gradually it was grasped that not only destruction but production would have to be organized on a scale never before attempted or imagined. The convoy system for shipping, the conscription of recruits, the rationing of food and direct government control of the railways, coal mines and munitions industry were all to prove essential steps in the process of mobilizing the nation to fight a total war. The conduct of Britain's war effort after 1939 was, therefore, based to a very great extent on the lessons so painfully learned after 1914.

BE PREPARED

The measures to be taken in the event of large-scale aerial bombing of civilians were being discussed by government committees as early as 1924. In 1935, only two years after Hitler came to power, the government sent a circular to local authorities, urging them to start drawing up their own ARP (Air

CHURCHMAN'S CIGARETTES

THE CIVILIAN RESPIRATOR—HOW TO ADJUST IT

WILLS'S CIGARETTES

THE CIVILIAN DUTY RESPIRATOR

WILLS'S CIGARETTES

A HEAVY ANTI-GAS SUIT

Coloured cards, given free in packets of cigarettes, gave instructions on how to survive air raids.

> **Every aspect of national life was regimented; nothing was so trivial that it did not become a cause for official concern. By the end of the war the government absorbed 60 per cent of all production; a third of personal expenditure was on items covered by rationing.**
>
> *Philip Ziegler, English historian — Elizabeth's Britain (1986)*

Raid Precautions) arrangements. The Munich crisis of 1938 gave officials of the London County Council the chance to test out their planned evacuation procedure on a limited scale by preparing to move some 4,000 pupils from its 'special schools' to the relative safety of the countryside. At the same time 38 million gas masks were hastily assembled and distributed to the public — a triumph of foresight which also brought home, as no other gesture perhaps could have done, that war was no longer a vague possibility but an imminent threat.

By the time war actually broke out in September 1939 ration books had already been printed for every household. Street lighting was extinguished and the use of car headlamps banned, with the result that road deaths doubled in a month and by the end of the year a fifth of the entire population claimed to have suffered some sort of accident or injury as a result of the 'blackout'. New ministries were established to handle the new tasks that the government would have to take on — Economic Warfare, to blockade the enemy; Shipping, to organize convoys and build ships to offset inevitable losses; Supply, to procure uniforms and munitions for the army; and Food, to organize rationing. Later on came a special Ministry of Aircraft Production under press-baron Lord Beaverbrook, to streamline the output of the most vital weapon for home defence — the fighter 'plane.

BRINGING IN THE EXPERTS

It was also realized that experts of every kind could make a vital contribution. University mathematicians were set to inventing and breaking secret codes and communication ciphers. Linguists reduced the English language to 27 verbs and 800 other words so that Poles and Czechs could learn 'Basic

DON'T YOU KNOW THERE'S A WAR ON?

English' in a month and be trained as fighter pilots. Stage-designers learned how to turn their skills to camouflaging everything from a tank to a factory. Research scientists were set to perfecting radar. Society photographer Cecil Beaton found himself taking pictures of pilots for a morale-boosting book about the RAF. Nutrition expert Professor Jack Drummond left University College, London to become chief scientific adviser in charge of the nation's diet. Refugee Hungarian movie producer Alexander Korda turned out a pro-British propaganda film 'The Lion Has Wings' in less than a month.

PROPAGANDA

Propaganda was the special responsibility of a new Ministry of Information, housed in the impressive but still uncompleted Senate House building of the University of London. Realizing that this time the war would not be 'over by Christmas' and that the civilian population would be subjected to many terrors and hardships, the government understood the need to provide the public with clear guidance on how to support the war effort and to sustain morale against false rumours, panic and despair.

> **. . . the interests about which workers in the industrial areas would want to talk are – the war, home politics, industrial grievances, football and the dogs. We believe that the kind of things they would want to say about the first three could not be broadcast.**
>
> *Director of BBC Scotland*

The Ministry's other tasks included trying to win neutral countries over to the British side and to counter enemy propaganda.

Don't forget that walls have ears!

CARELESS TALK COSTS LIVES

A campaign involving 2·5 million posters tried to reverse traditional British attitudes towards the right of 'free speech'.

These tasks involved close liaison with BBC radio, which was correctly perceived as the most powerful medium of mass-communication.

> **The BBC's pioneer TV broadcasts, begun in 1936, were suspended for the duration of the war for fear that signals might provide navigational aid to enemy bombers.**

Although publication of the Communist 'Daily Worker' was suppressed most newspapers were given a fairly free hand. Only if they published pictures, cartoons and opinions which strayed outside government guidelines were they reprimanded – after the event.

THE 'PHONEY WAR'

Ironically the war, so long prepared for, was initially experienced as an anti-climax. Britain's declaration of war on Germany on 3 September 1939 was provoked by Germany's attack on Poland, whose security Britain had pledged to uphold. In practice there was almost nothing Britain actually could do to help Poland, whose forces fought bravely but hopelessly against overwhelmingly better-armed forces. Within three weeks organized Polish resistance had been crushed. After that, winter closed in and active campaigning was suspended until the following spring. Americans came to call this period 'the phoney war' but at the time British people were more likely to call it 'the bore war'.

Preventing illness was seen as a contribution to a healthy and hard-working labour force.

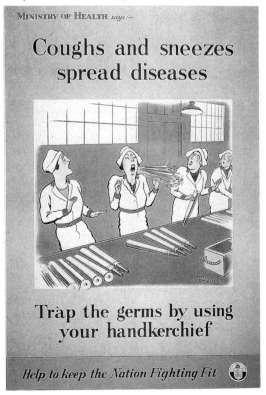

MINISTRY OF HEALTH *says:—*

Coughs and sneezes spread diseases

Trap the germs by using your handkerchief

Help to keep the Nation Fighting Fit

THE EDGE OF DEFEAT

The spring of 1940 saw a sudden and terrible resumption of Nazi aggression, but this time in the West. The German forces' *Blitzkrieg* ('lightning war') tactics made novel and skilful use of close co-ordination between aircraft and highly-mechanized ground forces. Striking suddenly, moving rapidly from one key objective to the next, the German invaders reduced their opponents' communications to chaos, flooding the roads with panic-stricken refugees and demoralizing the confused and isolated bodies of troops who tried to fight back. The low-lying countries of Belgium, the Netherlands and Denmark fell within weeks. Mountainous Norway, supported by a British amphibious landing, took a little longer to overrun. The failure of British assistance to Norway led to a fierce debate in Parliament which brought down Neville Chamberlain's Conservative government and led to its replacement by a coalition under Winston Churchill.

Almost as soon as Churchill took power he was faced by the collapse of Britain's chief ally, as France negotiated a separate peace with Germany and allowed German forces to occupy its coastline. With the extraordinary aid of 700 'little ships', ranging from family cabin-cruisers to river paddle-steamers, the bulk of the ill-fated British Expeditionary Force was evacuated from the beaches of Dunkirk in Northern France, along with more than 100,000 French troops.

> **For a good look at how ordinary people felt about the war, read Don't You Know There's a War On, listed in Further Reading.**

All Britain now waited for invasion. Apart from the dominions and colonies of the empire, who could send little in the way of armed support, the 'Mother Country' stood alone. A successful cross-Channel invasion would, however, require temporary air superiority which, in August and September, the fighter pilots of the Luftwaffe attempted to gain. They lost the 'Battle of Britain' and German tactics switched to bombing London and other major ports and industrial cities throughout the winter of 1940–41.

This offensive ended when Hitler diverted his air force to support his invasion of the Soviet Union in the spring of 1941. The invasion of Britain was no longer an immediate danger and the real possibility of crushing defeat began to recede.

When Japan attacked the US Pacific naval base at Pearl Harbor in December 1941 the United States at last turned from being a supportive neutral to a whole-hearted ally, though it would take months for her vast industrial strength to be switched over to war-production.

THE LONG SLOG

If victory, in the long run, at least seemed certain it must still be remembered that, until 1942, the number of British civilians killed by enemy bombing exceeded the number of British servicemen killed hitting back at the enemy. Bad news continued to roll in – the Japanese capture of Singapore, allegedly impregnable bastion of British power in the Far East; reverses in North Africa; continued shipping losses in the Atlantic; a disastrous Canadian commando raid on Dieppe.

Only with General Montgomery's great victory over the legendary Rommel in October 1942, at the ten-day battle of El Alamein in North Africa, came the first undoubted British success of the war – after three years. Throughout the nation church bells – which were to be the signal that

> . . . we children at home are full of cheerfulness and courage. We are trying to do all we can to help . . . and . . . to bear our own share of the danger and sadness of war. We know, every one of us, that in the end all will be well.
>
> *Princess Elizabeth, aged 14 – BBC radio broadcast to children overseas, October 1940*

invasion had begun – were rung in celebration.

After that the war entered its final phase, a long slog to open up a 'Second Front' to complement the efforts of the Soviet Union, now driving Nazi forces out of its territory. In 1943, having cleared North Africa of Axis (i.e. German and Italian) forces, the British and Americans invaded Europe from the south via Sicily, but became bogged down in Italy, even though the Italians switched to the Allied side. In June 1944 the invasion of Normandy, a thrust into Europe from the north, was launched from the largest invasion fleet ever assembled in the history of warfare. After liberating France and other conquered countries the Allies aimed to push on into Germany to 'shake hands with the Russians' moving in from the East.

There were still set-backs – the totally unexpected V-1 and V-2 rocket bombing campaigns, the German winter counter-offensive in the Ardennes, the failure of the airborne attempt to seize the Rhine bridges at Arnhem. But the prospect of victory was solid enough to set civilians and servicemen alike talking about what sort of Britain they wanted after the war.

The defeat of Nazi Germany was achieved in May 1945. Churchill approved a brief period of rejoicing but reminded the cheering crowds that there was another victory yet to be won – in the East, against Japan. The

Apart from paying 50 per cent of their earnings in income tax and buying war savings certificates citizens were encouraged to make further financial contributions to a war that cost £11 million a day in its first year.

general feeling was that this would take another eighteen months and might cost a million more Allied lives.

In the event it was achieved by August as a result of the dropping of two atomic bombs. The very existence of such horrendous weapons was perhaps among the best-kept of the war's many secrets. By that time

Winston Churchill, saviour of his country, had been dismissed from office by the British electorate and a reforming Labour government elected by a landslide. It was a striking demonstration of the power of the democracy which the war had been fought to defend.

11

A NATION IN ARMS

FROM VOLUNTEERS TO CONSCRIPTS

Before the First World War Britain had always prided itself on having an all-volunteer army. Conscription of young men for compulsory military service was the general rule in continental countries; but most British people thought this was unworthy of a free nation. The national crisis of the First World War put this belief to a supreme test and for two years the flow of volunteers to the colours was sufficient to fill the rapidly expanding ranks of Kitchener's 'New Army'. Not until the summer of 1916 was it necessary to pass a law making military service compulsory.

Even before the conflict was over, however, it was gradually realized that a system of purely voluntary recruitment had grave drawbacks from the point of view of managing the overall conduct of the war efficiently. Skilled men who would have been more effectively employed turning out vital munitions and equipment in the factories were lying dead in France. Had recruitment been compulsory from the first, men could have been directed to where they could make the best contribution or kept in 'reserved occupations'. It was a hard lesson to learn; but it was not forgotten. As war loomed in the 1930s

preparation for compulsory mobilization of the country's manpower began with a scheme of national registration of men of military age, which was defined as 18–41.

CIVILIANS IN UNIFORM

When Lord Kitchener, Secretary for War, had called for an army of a million men in 1914, civilians found the idea of such a vast armed force difficult to take in. By 1918, however, some five million Britons were in uniform. The outbreak of the Second World War, by contrast, saw a population fully aware that the services would have to expand to ten times or more their peacetime strength.

The population of quiet rural areas quickly became accustomed to the establishment of training camps and the arrival of hundreds of young recruits. They were welcomed not only for patriotic reasons but because the camps often created new jobs in construction and bought local farm produce. Servicemen spent their spare cash in local pubs and shops and organized dances and sports which brought a new liveliness that local young people much appreciated. On the other hand, military exercises often disrupted local life and transport and sometimes damaged farmland and public facilities.

Many of these men were destined to fight

Prime Minister Churchill (left, with stick) is cheered as he tours a bombed-out area of Manchester.

overseas — in the deserts of North Africa, the mountains of Italy, the orchards of Normandy or the jungles of Burma. Some were posted abroad for more than five years continuously. But hundreds of thousands were assigned to home-based services.

By the end of the war some half a million women had joined the armed services. Most served as drivers or did clerical work but

The vast mass of London itself, fought street by street, could easily devour an entire hostile army and we would rather see London laid in ashes and ruins than that it should be tamely and abjectly enslaved.

Winston Churchill, 14 July 1940

13

> **There isn't a single record of any British women in uniformed service quitting her post, or failing in her duty under fire. When you see a girl in uniform with a bit of ribbon on her tunic, remember that she didn't get it for knitting more socks than anyone else . . .**
>
> *Booklet issued to US troops arriving in Britain*

many also did technical jobs. There were, for example, a thousand all-woman barrage-balloon crews. The ATS recruited the largest number — 198,000, followed by the WAAF, 171,000 and then the WRNS, 74,000. Although women were not trained for face-to-face combat many did learn to use firearms and thousands actually served with anti-aircraft batteries.

FIGHTING FROM BELOW

Aerial warfare created the need for new defensive services. The Royal Observer Corps was trained to give early warning of incoming enemy planes. Anti-aircraft crews manned not only guns but also searchlights and barrage balloons. The Coast Guard and lifeboat men were constantly on alert for 'ditched' pilots and torpedoed seamen. In London alone the Fire Brigade increased its strength by the addition of 20,000 Auxiliary Fire Service (AFS) volunteers to the ranks of the 2,000 peacetime regulars.

They were only part of a larger team which included Civil Defence, whose main responsibility was ARP; heavy rescue and demolition squads, who got people out of blitzed buildings and pulled down unsafe ones; and the Women's Voluntary Service (WVS), a million-strong army of mums and aunties in green greatcoats who helped in the rest centres where the homeless were sheltered, and manned the tea-stalls which kept the emergency services going through long hours of back-breaking work.

Less glamorous, but no less essential to the task of keeping the war effort going were the contributions of transport workers, postmen and technicians in the gas, water, telephone and electricity services who had to run and repair whatever the bombing had disrupted or destroyed.

A Home Guard contingent. Note the gas-masks, slung in pouches, worn on the chest.

THE HOME GUARD

In the summer of 1940, under the threat of immediate invasion, the government called on men who (by reason of age or occupation) were outside the scope of the 'call-up', to enroll as Local Defence Volunteers. Within twenty-four hours a quarter of a million had done so. The members of what later became known as 'Dad's Army' made up in keenness what they lacked in equipment. Armed with shotguns and broomsticks, at first they had to make do with arm-bands rather than uniforms.

> **The Home Guard harassed innocent civilians for identity cards, put up primitive road-blocks . . . and sometimes made bombs out of petrol tins. In a serious invasion, its members would presumably have been massacred if they had managed to assemble at all.**
>
> A. J. P. Taylor, English historian – English History 1914–45 (1965)

Often the target of humorous scorn (LDV = Look, Duck and Vanish), they gradually gained in both public esteem and numbers. Within a month Churchill had renamed them the 'Home Guard'. Half a million rifles were swiftly procured for them from America.

At their peak stength, in 1943, the Home Guard numbered 1,175,000 – twice as many as the home-based regulars. The theory was that, having a detailed knowledge of their own towns and villages, they would act as a first line of defence against invaders, skirmishing to hold them up while regular forces assembled to counter-attack. Fortunately this was never put to the test. But they did useful service in rounding up 'downed' Luftwaffe pilots and guarding bridges, power-

This sixteen year-old despatch-rider was the first Home Guard member to be mentioned in despatches for bravery. Although blown off his bike by blast he ran almost a mile through a raid to deliver his message.

stations and other installations, thus releasing regular troops for more demanding tasks.

A ROYAL EXAMPLE

While Churchill offered a kind of leadership which was both aggressive and flamboyant, the Royal Family set an example of quiet conscientiousness. The King, shy and stammering, was ill-fitted by temperament to

15

The Queen and King, third and fourth from left, watch Princess Elizabeth, far right, receive instruction on how to crank-start a car.

public occasions but travelled tirelessly visiting camps, hospitals, factories and fortifications. He covered over half a million miles within the UK alone, as well as making five trips to overseas theatres of war. Himself a Great War veteran, having fought at the Battle of Jutland in 1916 and qualified as a pilot in 1918, he always appeared in uniform, wearing the dress of the army, navy and air force in rotation. At Buckingham Palace or in the field he personally decorated over 33,000 men and women for acts of bravery and devotion to duty. In 1940 he instituted a new award, the George Cross, to stand beside the Victoria Cross (for combatants) as a special decoration for civilians who displayed outstanding courage in situations of great danger.

> **The children can't go without me. I can't leave the King and of course the King won't go.**
>
> *The Queen, 1939*

Other members of the Royal Family also played their part. The Queen (who wore civilian clothes but took revolver lessons) put special emphasis on touring bombed areas and pioneered the 'walkabout', plunging into crowds of bemused bystanders to hear about their experiences for herself. Princess Elizabeth (the present Queen) joined the ATS as soon as she reached eighteen and qualified as a driver. The Duke of Kent served in the RAF and was the first member of the Royal Family to die on active service when his plane disappeared on a flight from Scotland to Iceland.

OUT OF STEP

There were also those who refused to serve. There was far less general hostility to 'conscientious objectors' than there had been in the First World War. And there was perhaps also a grudging acknowledgment that a country fighting against tyranny and in defence of liberty was more or less bound to respect the conscience of the individual citizen. But the fate of any particular 'CO' was an uncertain one as the decisions of exemption tribunals varied greatly from one part of the country to another. At one, in Bristol, more than half of those who appeared before it were granted exemptions, at another, in London, none were. In all 50,000 men and 2,000 women registered as COs. Of these 2,900 were given unconditional exemptions. The overwhelming majority were given conditional exemptions which enabled them to serve in hospitals, in the emergency services

or on the land. Those who refused any sort of service which might aid the war effort, about 5,000, were prosecuted and most of them sent to prison.

Aliens born in enemy countries were interned. Most of the nominal Germans and Austrians were Jewish refugees or political opponents of the Nazis who had fled to Britain for safety. Now they were locked up with pro-Nazis and suspected spies and saboteurs. The bulk were shipped off to the Isle of Man where they were sorted into three categories — those who were regarded as a danger to public security and needed to be kept closely guarded; those who could be cleared to serve the war-effort, and those who needed further investigation until they could be assigned to one of the other two categories.

The Italian community, though it contained a few enthusiastic fascists, consisted mostly of hard-working cooks, waiters and owners of cafes and restaurants, most of whom had lived in Britain for many years and thought of it as their home. But they also fell victim to Churchill's order to 'collar the lot'. Hundreds were packed onto the Arandora Star bound for internment in Canada. Three hours after clearing Liverpool on 1 July 1940 the liner was torpedoed by a U-boat; 730 drowned, including 661 German and Italian internees.

> Conscientious objectors cause a good deal of heartburning . . . Many dismiss them all as unnatural and meet to be shot but the more thinking usually concede that it requires a good deal of guts to be a CO and that we have taken the easy way out by following the crowd.
>
> *Mass Observation report on RAF conscripts' views, April 1940*

> You, You and You! The People Out of Step with World War Two (listed in Further Reading) is a very interesting collection of the views of those people who refused to serve or who were imprisoned or deported during the war.

Pro-Nazi Britons were also imprisoned — 1,769 of them, including a Member of Parlia-

Just practising. Pre-invasion exercise for troops in a bombed-out area of London. Notice that the German 'prisoners' jackboots are in fact Wellingtons.

ment. Of these 763 were members of the British Union of Fascists, including its leader, former MP Sir Oswald Mosley. 1,106 of these British internees were later released as harmless, though Mosley himself was not freed until 1943. Even then Labour MPs criticized the move, though Churchill personally approved it.

The attitude of the Communists was inconsistent. Having unflinchingly opposed fascism, in Spain and elsewhere, in the 1930s,

the Communist Party at first denounced the war against Hitler as merely a struggle between capitalists and therefore irrelevant to the interests of the working class. A third of the membership resigned in protest. When Hitler turned to attack the USSR the Communist Party was suddenly obliged to reverse its attitude and call for all out effort in support of the war. Though there was later widespread British admiration for the heroism of the Red Army the general attitude to

Britain's own homegrown Communists wavered between suspicion and scorn.

BANNED!

5 June 1940	**Strikes**
10 July 1940	**British Union of Fascists**
20 July 1940	**Buying or selling new cars**
8 January 1941	**Communist newspaper 'Daily Worker'**
11 March 1942	**White bread**
31 July 1942	**Motoring for pleasure**
1 April 1944	**Visits to within ten miles of coast from the Wash to Land's End**
27 April 1944	**Travel abroad**

BRITAIN OCCUPIED!

One area of the UK presented a special case. The Channel Islands were the only part of the British Isles actually to endure Nazi occupation. About a quarter of the population, including most of the men of military age, took advantage of the offer of evacuation before June 1940. The rest chose to await the invader and sit it out.

We often hear about the food situation and envy the fortunate people in England.

Guernsey farmer, October 1941

Beyond persistent thieving and 'losing'

tools, equipment, spare parts etc., there was no organized resistance, though secret listening to the BBC on homemade 'crystal-sets' was widespread, in defiance of German orders. Everything was in short supply, except tomatoes (the islands' main crop) and paper (to wrap the tomatoes in). Standards of diet and clothing were far worse than in mainland Britain but, if there was more discomfort, there was less actual danger.

The German occupation forces enforced a strict curfew, issued many petty regulations and confiscated most vehicles and supplies. They did, however, also behave with great correctness towards the civilian populaton and punished severely any criminal acts by German soldiers. On Alderney, which was virtually cleared of its civilian population, the occupiers ran a slave-labour camp populated by thousands of Russian, Polish and other prisoners-of-war. An unknown number were done to death, either deliberately or as a result of their harsh treatment.

. . . In the Channel Islands British citizens, however unwillingly, raised food to feed German troops, built emplacements for German guns and oiled ammunition for use in invading the British Isles.

Norman Longmate, English historian – How We Lived Then (1971)

As the public records relating to the occupation of the Channel Islands are to remain sealed until the year 2045 it is currently impossible to learn much more about these and other atrocities, or indeed to discover how many islanders anonymously denounced their neighbours to the occupiers for breaches of regulations – or went further and actively collaborated with the Nazis.

THE ENEMY ABOVE

THINGS TO COME

In the 1936 film of H. G. Wells' science-fiction novel *Things to Come* British cinema-goers were given a foretaste of what modern warfare might mean for the average civilian. The opening sequence shows a busy street, thronged with happy shoppers. Suddenly there is a drone of aircraft engines. A bomb drops. People scream and, panic-stricken, run madly in all directions. A bus swerves from the road and plunges through the plate-glass window of a department store. Bodies are crushed under falling masonry . . .

The 'movie-fan' could draw some comfort from the fact that it was 'only a film' – but the newsreels would soon show the destruction of the Spanish town of Guernica by Germany's Condor Legion and the massacre of Chinese civilians in Shanghai by the Japanese air-force.

A.R.P.

Hitler's well-publicised efforts to build up his Luftwaffe (Air Weapon) prompted Parliament to pass an 'Air Raid Precautions Act' in 1937, obliging local authorities to plan how they could reduce or repair the effects of enemy action against the civil population. In March 1938 Home Secretary Sir Samuel Hoare

appealed for at least a million men and women for work that in an emergency would be exciting and dangerous. Less than half the necessary number of volunteers were forthcoming. The Munich crisis of 1938 brought a new urgency to the situation and the publication of an official pamphlet on 'The Protection of Your Home Against Air Raids'. Suddenly the ARP had more volunteers than its instructors could handle. The air raid warden, male or female, formed the backbone of the civil defence system, and was trained to recognize poison gas, give first aid, direct people to shelter and assist the rescue services.

In July 1939 a new Civil Defence Act increased local government powers to build shelters, take over buildings and improve plans for evacuation and firefighting. All firms employing over 30 people had to organize ARP training. And, as an additional measure, by September 1939 two million steel 'Anderson' shelters (named after Sir John Anderson, Home Secretary) had been distributed.

THE BLITZ

A year was to pass, however, before the deliberate mass-bombing of civilians began – and then it was revealed how mistaken many of the careful preparations had been. Planners

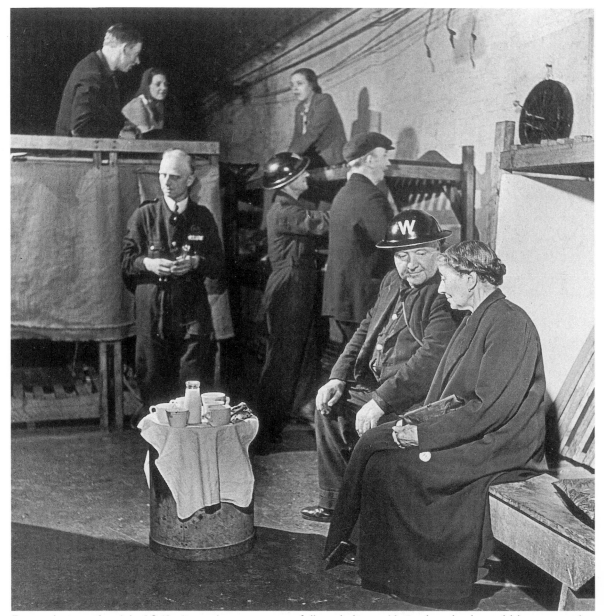

Tea and sympathy, July 1941. A warden reassures a fellow-shelterer. Notice how bunks could be screened off for privacy.

had assumed that the greatest danger would come from daylight raiders dropping gas-bombs – hence the priority given to radar so that they could be detected and intercepted and the investment in gas-masks to protect the civilian population.

BOTH SIDES AGREE NOT TO BOMB CIVILIANS

Washington Post, 3 September 1939

21

THE ENEMY ABOVE

In the event gas was never used and instead night-time raiders dropped high-explosive and incendiary bombs. Suddenly it was realized that what was needed were more barrage balloons (to force raiders to fly high and lose accuracy); more searchlights (to pick out targets for ack-ack crews); more shelters for the civilian population; better co-ordination of fire crews to stop fires spreading; and the creation of 'heavy rescue' squads with the skills and equipment to get people out of bombed buildings.

> **We are all in the 'Front Line' and we realize it.**
>
> *Henry Penny, London Bus Driver, September 1940*

The first large-scale German raid was on London – after the failure of the Luftwaffe's efforts to destroy RAF fighter strength in the Battle of Britain. Churchill had warned before the war that 'the flying peril is not one from which we can fly. We cannot move London.' It was an obvious target for many reasons – the seat of government, which co-ordinated the whole war-effort; the nation's greatest port and the largest concentration of civilian population – and also the city whose survival or destruction would be most closely noted by every neutral or allied power. To attack London was to attack Britain itself.

> **The treasures of the National Gallery were stored in a disused slate quarry in North Wales and the British Museum's sculptures in a disused London tram-tunnel. The best china from Buckingham Palace was stored in Aldwych Underground station.**

The thin steel of an 'Anderson' shelter, when screened with a mound of protective earth, could stand almost anything but a direct hit.

On the afternoon of 7 September 1940 a force of 375 German planes attacked London; a second wave came in that night, guided by the fires the first wave had started. By dawn the next day sixty major fires — any one of them large enough to make peace-time head-lines — were still raging and 430 Londoners were dead.

> **Nobody foresaw the tidal wave of refugees spread all over the country after the first hideous weekend, inundating places like Oxford with homeless people, being decanted in peaceful Essex suburbs from lorries by desperate local authorities. . . Nobody foresaw . . . the rest centres would be overflowing, that people would stay there for weeks instead of hours . . . that transport would not turn up, so that refugees were bombed to death in the rest centres . . .**
>
> *Mass Observation, 1940*

By the end of September 5,730 had been killed and over 10,000 seriously injured. The raids continued for the next fifty-seven nights non-stop. In November there were three nights without raids. They finally stopped in May 1941. St. Paul's Cathedral, Buckingham Palace and Westminster Abbey were all hit but, thanks to the prompt action of fire-watchers, suffered no irreparable damage. Guildhall and the House of Commons were damaged so badly that they could

> **I'm glad we've been bombed. It makes me feel I can look the East End in the face.**
>
> *The Queen, September 1940*

not be repaired until after the war. Many of Wren's beautiful churches were completely destroyed.

Over 170,000 people took shelter down 'the Tube', but they represented only 5 per cent of the total population of the capital. Nor did the Underground guarantee safety — there were six hundred casualties at Balham when a bomb tore through water mains and sewers to launch a tidal wave of sludge along the platform and a hundred died at Bank when it also suffered a direct hit. Many more people took their chances in shelters and no less than sixty per cent stayed in their houses — under the stairs, under the kitchen table or in bed.

> **In the infernos of the Underground the poor wretches take up their positions for the night's sleep at four o'clock in the afternoon. The winter must surely bring epidemics of flu, even typhoid.**
>
> *Cecil Beaton, photographer, October 1940*

> **. . . people don't go to the tubes merely for extra safety . . . harassed housewives found that they could halve their housework if the family spent the main part of its leisure time . . . somewhere other than in the home . . . some found themselves possessed of unsuspected talents for organizing, entertaining . . . which for the first time found scope and appreciation.**
>
> *Mass Observation, 1943*

In November the Germans began to bomb two dozen other major ports and industrial centres, starting with Coventry where over 500 died and the medieval cathedral was gutted. (Nevertheless the city's factories

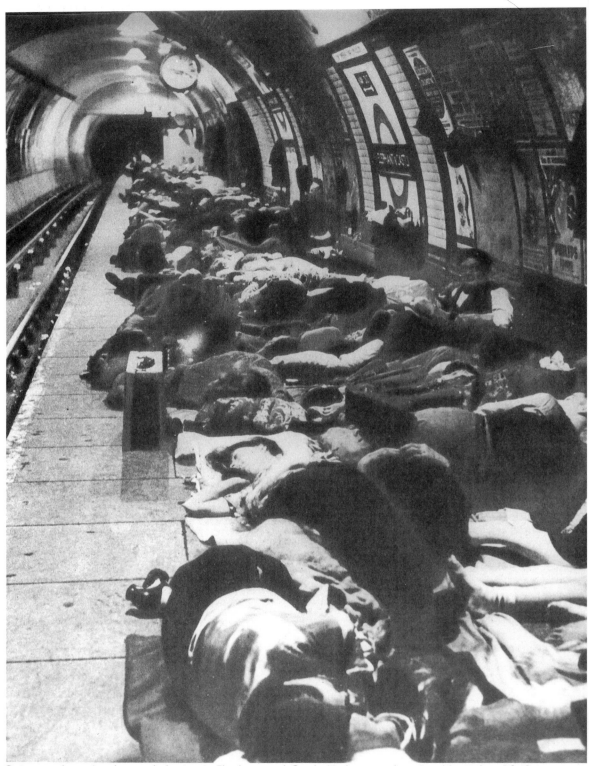

Going nowhere. Londoners sheltering in Elephant and Castle Underground station, November 1940.

were back in full production five days later.) The damage at Bristol shocked visiting officials from London. After the raid on Plymouth 50,000 people trekked out to sleep in the countryside each night.

> **They don't laugh at wardens any more . . . We are policemen, nurses, fire-fighters, watchers for danger . . . and give comfort and confidence to all . . .**
>
> *Stanley Lupino, Actor & ARP warden, October 1940*

At Birmingham, the last major city to be raided, over 2,000 were killed, four times as many as in Coventry. In terms of homelessness the worst place to suffer was Clydebank in Scotland where two thirds of the population lost the roof over their heads. The total death-toll for the Blitz was around 30,000 more than half of which was accounted for by London. But for every civilian killed thirty-five were made homeless as 3.5 million houses were destroyed or damaged.

> **Gas, light and water were off in most parts of the town (Southampton) . . . The army was demolishing buildings . . . AFS (Auxiliary Fire Service) men had come from as far as Oxford, Northampton, Hove . . . Police had also been drafted in . . . this caused much confusion, as people were asking the police the way and the police had no idea.**
>
> *Mass Observation, December 1940*

BAEDEKER RAIDS

In the spring of 1942 the RAF attacked the historic German cities of Lubeck and Col-

ogne. The Germans retaliated with what came to be called the Baedeker raids — named after a famous tourist guidebook. These picked out equally historic British cities such as York, Canterbury, Norwich, Bath and Exeter, which suffered worst of all. Oxford was spared because Hitler wanted to make it the capital after he conquered Britain.

'V' WEAPONS

Another mini-blitz occurred in the spring of 1943 but the last major onslaught did not take place until the summer of 1944 with the arrival of the first 'V-bombs'. (Vergeltungswaffen — revenge weapons). The V-1, nicknamed the 'doodlebug', was a jet-powered pilotless plane which travelled at 400 mph, carrying a ton of high explosive, and, when over its target area, cut its engine to spiral down and detonate.

> **The first thing which the rescue squads and the firemen saw . . . was . . . shadowy men . . . crouching over any dead or wounded woman . . . and ripping off its necklace, or earrings, or brooch, rifling its handbag . . .**
>
> *Novelist Nicholas Monsarrat describing the bombing of the Cafe de Paris, Piccadilly, March 1941*

It was scarcely an accurate weapon, having a target radius of fifteen miles. And of the 244 launched against London in the first major attack on 15 June 1944 only 72 reached the city. By feeding false reports to the Germans British intelligence managed to get them to adjust their ranging so that the missiles fell consistently short of the centre of the capital. (With the unfortunate result that three-quarters of all Croydon's houses were to be damaged.) The RAF's 426 mph Tem-

Rescued! – over 10,000 lives were saved by skilled rescue squads.

pest fighters learned to upset the V-1's gyro-steering system with the slipstream of their wings by flying right in front of them and thus accounted for a third of incoming missiles.

Barrage balloons took down more. By relocating London's anti-aircraft defences along the south coast (1,000 guns and 23,000 personnel were moved in four days) it eventually proved possible to bring down six out of every seven launched. As the advancing Allied armies captured the V-1 launch-sites the campaign petered out in September 1944, having inflicted 6,184 deaths and 17,981 serious injuries.

One more terror remained, the even more powerful V-2, a 12 ton rocket against which there was no effective defence. Travelling at 4,000 mph it would be in flight for less than

> **For a dog or cat . . . the blitz must have been a hundred times worse than being let loose on Guy Fawkes night . . . a dog or cat's hearing and sensitivity to vibration are far more acute than our own . . . animal welfare societies . . . between 1939 and 1945 rescued an incredible 256,000 animals and birds from bombing raids.**
>
> *Jilly Cooper, English writer – Animals in War (1983)*

four minutes and would strike without warning or possibility of interception. Five hundred hit London between September 1944 and the capture of their bases in March 1945, killing 2,724 and injuring 6,746.

WE'LL MEET AGAIN

EVACUATION

In the course of the entire war over 60 million people notified official changes of address, which was as though the entire population had moved home at least once and a third had done so twice.

The first great wave of movement was caused by the long-planned evacuation from major cities of children under fifteen, pregnant mothers, mothers of children under five and the blind and severely disabled. Not only did this remove the most vulnerable from the risk of bombing, it also cleared schools which could now be used as Rest Centres and ARP posts and vacated hospital beds for the reception of casualties. Originally government plans intended to move some four million individuals but when it came to it they shifted rather less than half that number. About two million people made their own private arrangements.

Most children went in school groups. Departures appear to have been fairly well organized but the reception areas were often chaotic. Parents were not notified of their children's destination until after they had arrived at it, sometimes several days after, which caused much worry and distress. Most children received a warm welcome but many were upset by a 'cattle-market' sort of pro-

> The purpose of evacuation is to remove from the crowded and vulnerable centres, if an emergency should arise, those, more particularly the children, whose presence cannot be of any assistance. Everyone will realize that there can be no question of wholesale clearance. We are not going to win a war by running away.
>
> *Civil Defence leaflet, July 1939 – 'Evacuation Why and How'*

cedure during which they were assembled in a school or village hall and picked out by their prospective foster-mothers. The scruffiest were usually left to last and sometimes had to be compulsorily 'billeted' on unwilling hosts.

'A PERPLEXING SOCIAL EVENT'

Within days, from every area to which evacuees had been sent, came cries of anger and anguish as countryfolk discovered that many of the town children had head-lice and skin diseases such as scabies and impetigo. A high proportion were prone to bedwetting.

One of the classic pictures of the war – children shelter in a field slit-trench as Nazi raiders fly over Kent. This picture was widely used in the USA to alert the public to the need to support Britain so that such scenes might not be repeated in America.

For many, no doubt, this was a nervous reaction to strange surroundings, but for some it was simply another result of their complete lack of basic toilet-training. Persistent swearing, lying and stealing were other complaints. Worse still was said about accompanying mothers who complained that villages without shops and cinemas were 'boring' and many of whom proved no cleaner and much more troublesome and ungrateful than the worst of the children.

Within a fortnight the House of Commons was discussing the impact of the evacuations as its main item of business.

> **Their clothing was in a deplorable condition, some of the children being literally sewn into their ragged little garments. Except for a small number the children were filthy, and in this district we have never seen so many verminous children, lacking any knowledge of clean and hygienic habits.**
>
> *Town Children through Country Eyes, 1940*

> **Much ill feeling has been caused . . . not between the rich and the poor but between the urban and the rural poor. This is a perplexing social event . . . but the effect will be to demonstrate to people how deplorable is the standard of life and civilization among the urban proletariat.**
>
> *Harold Nicolson, MP, October 1939*

WHAT IS TO BE DONE?

So widespread and so deep was the reaction against evacuees that the National Federation of Women's Institutes was soon formally deploring certain conditions of English town life as disclosed by evacuation and asking that remedies should be sought.

One outcome of this was 'Our Towns: A Close-Up', published in 1943 as a result of an enquiry of an all-women's committee chaired by Margaret Bondfield, who had been Britain's first woman Cabinet minister.

'Our Towns' did not mince words. While making it clear that complaints 'related to only a small proportion of the evacuees' it also emphasized that 'they were nationwide and concerned some of those from every area evacuated'. From a national point of view, the report said, the evacuees who were complained about constituted a community that was 'a hidden sore, poor, dirty and crude in its habits, an intolerable and degrading burden to decent people forced by poverty to neighbour with it.'

Among the remedies the report called for were: more nursery schools 'where habits can be formed, health and nutrition safeguarded'; better educational and recreational facilities in slum areas; more health visitors and clinics; tougher punishments for neglectful parents; and 'a square-toothed steel nit-comb . . . at a price within the reach of all.'

> **Wartime schooling was badly disrupted because**
> - **many city schools were closed by evacuation and others were bombed out**
> - **country schools were overcrowded with refugees**
> - **trained teachers were recruited into the services**
> - **books and paper were in very short supply**

Something hot to keep you going. Field-ovens provided hot drinks, soups and stews which brought comfort and renewed energy to exhausted and confused victims of bombing.

For many mothers and children evacuation proved to be only a brief interlude. Homesickness, the fear of wives for husbands, the frictions between disillusioned 'hosts' and discontented 'guests' and the fact that no air-raids were happening all combined to entice half or more of the evacuees back to the cities by Christmas. With the onset of the 'Blitz' in the autumn of 1940 evacuation schemes were reactivated and once again over a million left the cities for the safety of the countryside. A further wave went in 1944 in response to the V-bomb attacks. Some of those who had gone in 1939, however, stayed for the whole six years — and some for the rest of their lives.

ABSENCE MAKES THE HEART GROW FONDER?

Even without the separations brought about by evacuation family life was badly strained by the absence in the forces of 2.5 million husbands and by the long hours worked in factories by wives and older daughters. Being 'bombed out' often deprived people of the support of nearby relatives or trusted neighbours just when they needed them most. Husbands and wives, parents and children, sweethearts in love, were often separated for long periods, frequently knowing that their absent loved one might be in danger and equally frequently not knowing where they were.

> We'll meet again,
> Don't know where,
> Don't know when,
> But I know we'll meet again
> Some sunny day.

Such conditions meant enormous popularity for sentimental songs which put into words what so many people felt but could not say for themselves — 'Wish Me Luck as You Wave Me Goodbye', 'That Lovely

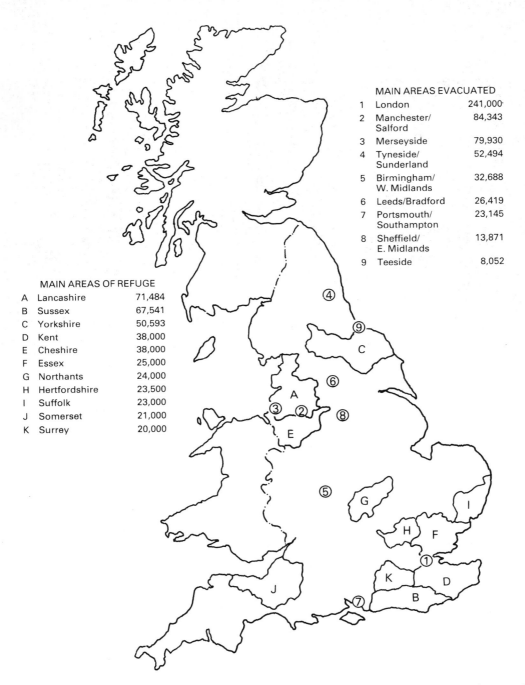

MAIN AREAS EVACUATED

1	London	241,000
2	Manchester/ Salford	84,343
3	Merseyside	79,930
4	Tyneside/ Sunderland	52,494
5	Birmingham/ W. Midlands	32,688
6	Leeds/Bradford	26,419
7	Portsmouth/ Southampton	23,145
8	Sheffield/ E. Midlands	13,871
9	Teeside	8,052

MAIN AREAS OF REFUGE

A	Lancashire	71,484
B	Sussex	67,541
C	Yorkshire	50,593
D	Kent	38,000
E	Cheshire	38,000
F	Essex	25,000
G	Northants	24,000
H	Hertfordshire	23,500
I	Suffolk	23,000
J	Somerset	21,000
K	Surrey	20,000

Weekend' and, most popular of all 'We'll Meet Again'.

OUT OF SIGHT, OUT OF MIND?

Absence from familiar surroundings, combined with large concentrations of young men and women in camps, hospitals and factories, also created situations where temptation was matched with opportunity. The real possibility of sudden death encouraged a 'live now, worry later' mentality. One result of this was a doubling of the number of people suffering from venereal diseases. (The

Vera Lynn — 'The Forces Sweetheart' — broadcasting from a BBC studio. Note the military-style cut of the jacket.

availability of penicillin from 1944 onwards provided a quick cure for the most common form of venereal disease, which meant that the armed forces were less seriously handicapped than they might otherwise have been.)

By 1942 the number of reported cases of venereal disease had risen by 70 per cent since 1939 to 70,000. Defence Regulation 33B then required anyone reported by two infected people as responsible for passing on the disease to be forced to have treatment. Dr Edith Summerskill MP estimated the true figure at 150,000 (more than the number of Blitz casualties) and called for even tougher measures.

> ... only those contacts who are informed upon by two infected patients will be obliged to submit to treatment. What of the others? There are a large number of innocent women infected by their husbands who will transmit venereal disease to their children but who will remain untreated because no informer will be forthcoming ... I want compulsory notification and for the transmission of the disease to be made a penal offence.
>
> *Edith Summerskill MP in a letter to* The Times *November 1942*

Another result was a rise in the number of illegitimate births, from 26,574 in 1940 to 64,174 in 1945. These bare figures do not, however, tell the whole story. Many babies were born out of wedlock simply because the parents were separated when one or other of them was suddenly 'posted' before they could get married. The percentage of unmarried mothers under 25 actually fell during the war while the highest increase (41 per cent) was among the 30–35 age group.

One reason for the decline in the numbers of unmarried mothers under 25 was the more general availability of contraceptives; but another was a rush to the altar which meant that a third of the women who married for the first time during the war were under twenty-one. Often the honeymoon was followed immediately by years of separation which meant that reunion could all too swiftly be followed by divorce. In 1939 there had been 10,000 divorces. In 1945 there were nearly 25,000 and in 1946 even more.

These rates of illegitimacy and divorce are, however, extremely low compared with what has become accepted as normal in Britain nowadays.

MEDICINE AND HEALTH

Before the outbreak of war the provision of medical services was a huge muddle funded haphazardly by government and private insurance schemes and charitable and municipal hospitals. There were no accurate official statistics even for the number of hospitals, beds, doctors and nurses. The need to plan for massive casualties changed all this, creating an organized system which formed the basis for the post-war National Health Service.

Apart from caring for battle and bombing casualties hospitals still had to deal with the 'normal' flow of traffic and industrial injuries, infectious diseases and maternity cases. Shortage were sometimes acute, even of such basic items as surgeon's rubber gloves. Recruitment of trained personnel into front-line services' medical corps also meant shortage of staff, the ranks often being filled by Irish, American or Commonwealth volunteers. Despite these pressures German POWs were given equal treatment with British wounded, except that their officers, unlike Allied ones, were left on common wards with other ranks.

THE KITCHEN FRONT

FOOD AS A WEAPON OF WAR

A good diet is essential for energy, health and morale. The First World War had shown the importance of the 'Kitchen Front' in keeping up the nation's fighting spirit. Deficiency diseases like rickets appeared among the children of the poor. The fact that there were shortages in some parts of the country and not others caused discontent. In 1916 a Food Controller, Lord Devonport, was appointed to start a rationing scheme. He had a long experience of the grocery trade but was quite ignorant of the science of nutrition. The diet he recommended was only half what a man doing even light work would need. After he resigned a fair and sensible system was worked out, based on the advice of scientists.

Even before war began in 1939 the Board of Trade had set up a Food Defence Plans Department to draw up detailed schemes of rationing. A separate Ministry of Food was established five days after war was declared; it came to employ 50,000 officials. The Minister of Food, Lord Woolton, became a skilful broadcaster who realized the importance of appealing directly to housewives to 'do their bit'. He also gave his chief scientific adviser, Professor Drummond, the backing he needed.

Ministry of Food Wartime Priorities

1. Increased consumption of potatoes, oatmeal, cheese, carrots and green vegetables.

2. At least one pint of milk a day to be supplied to children under 15, expectant mothers and nursing mothers.

3. Vitamins A & D (which occur naturally in butter) to be added to margarine.

4. Extra calcium to be added to 'National Bread'.

RATIONING

Scarce foodstuffs, like fats and sugar, were to be distributed evenly but with special extra allowances to people with special needs. So men doing heavy work but who couldn't get a hot meal in a canteen (like miners) were allowed extra cheese for sandwiches. And children under five didn't qualify for a ration of tea but did get concentrated orange juice and cod-liver oil. Chocolate and raisins were allocated as energy rich snacks to bomber crews on long, cold flights.

Queueing became so much a part of the British way of life that people would join a queue as soon as they saw one and then ask what it was a queue for.

Although ration books had already been printed when the war broke out rationing was not introduced until an opinion poll showed that the public actually welcomed the idea. The system was ingenious, if rather complicated. Some basic foods (e.g. meat) were rationed by value and others (fats) by weight. The distribution of items which were too irregular in supply (coffee, pepper, imported canned goods) to be dealt with in either of these ways was regulated by a system of coupons known as 'points'. When stocks of a particular product appeared to be piling up in the warehouses its points value was lowered and when it was in short supply it was raised. Fish and offal were never rationed but were often difficult to get. Potatoes and bread were always available as fillers, though the bread was now coarse and 'dirty-looking' because more husk was ground into the flour. The result was more nutritious but less appetizing.

> **Those who have the will to win**
> **Cook potatoes in their skin**
> **For they know the sight of peelings**
> **Deeply hurts Lord Woolton's**
> **   feelings.**
>
> *Ministry of Food slogan*

Rationing was fair and fairly applied. But there was also a 'black market' which enabled those with the cash and the contacts to get special treats (lemons, jellies, whisky) for special occasions.

TOWN AND COUNTRY

Despite rationing country people usually had a better diet than city people. They had more space to grow vegetables – a quarter of London homes had no garden at all. They could keep bees and chickens. (In the 1930s the average Briton ate three eggs a week; during the war one a fortnight.) They could pick wild mushrooms and berries, catch fish and snare rabbits and pigeons for the pot. They were usually more skilled at making jams and chutneys.

> **Townspeople envied country folk their fresh eggs, milk, vegetables ... poultry, mutton and home-cured bacon. Country people ... rarely had the opportunity to supplement their rations with restaurant meals and frequently found that a consignment of off-the-ration goods in the nearest town had been snapped up by the locals before news of its arrival filtered out ...**
>
> *Sadie Ward — War in the Countryside (1988)*

Even the rich turned 'back to the land'. Lady Diana Cooper, wife of the Minister of Information, kept a cow at her country home and learned to milk it herself and make cheese. She also kept a goat, pigs, ducks and hens (yielding ten eggs a day). Her enterprise caused a minor sensation when she was prosecuted and fined for feeding stale bread to her livestock. (It should have gone into sausages or puddings for human consumption.)

'DIG FOR VICTORY'

The gap between town and country was narrowed by the 'Dig for Victory' campaign launched in October 1939. This encouraged townspeople to turn their lawns and flower-beds over to vegetables. The royal parks showed the way, turfing out geraniums in favour of cabbages. Even railway embankments and bombsites were taken into cultivation. The number of allotments in use rose from 815,000 in 1939 to 1,145,000 by 1942.

Local horticultural societies helped keen new gardeners learn from old hands.

> **Many people kept hens to boost the family egg ration. Consequently grain became short ... the RSPCA stepped in, suggesting that people should feed their chickens on weed seeds, berries and nuts, and drew up a leaflet telling people which seeds and berries were poisonous and which not.**
>
> *Jilly Cooper, English writer — Animals in War 1983*

Readers of 'Fur and Feather' learned that a diet of otherwise useless carrot tops, wall-flowers and lupins could turn a baby rabbit into two and a half pounds of meat and a pair of fur gloves for winter. Many firemen, with long hours to kill on duty, took to keeping pigs, fattened up on the waste from the station kitchen.

AGRICULTURE

Effort and enthusiasm could enhance the diet of an individual family but an efficient national food policy had to be guided by science. At first the Ministry of Agriculture wanted to expand meat production but the scientists of the Ministry of Food showed that for every acre devoted to fodder crops for livestock ten times as much food value could be produced if it were devoted to cereals for direct human consumption. As a result, four million acres were switched from livestock to arable between 1939 and 1941, saving 22 million tons of shipping space which would otherwise have been needed for imported cereals. The other priorities for British agricultural output were milk and vegetables, especially potatoes.

Over the course of the war the acreage under cultivation rose from 12 to 18 millions and the labour force increased by 20 per cent, with the gaps caused by service recruitment being filled by the 90,000 strong Women's Land Army, prisoners-of-war (130,000 Italians and 90,000 Germans) and the volunteer efforts of adults (80,000) and schoolchildren (70,000) at harvest time. In the 1930s home food production provided about 900 calories per head per day, some 30 per cent of the needed total; by the 1940s the figure had risen to 1,200, about 40 per cent.

IMPORTS

Imports therefore remained vital for feeding the nation and the application of science ensured that shipping space was used with the greatest efficiency by concentrating on foods with a high nutritional value in relation to their volume – cheese, canned fatty fish (e.g. mackerel) and pulses (beans, lentils) –

rather than 'exotic' fruits such as bananas or bulky, fragile ones, like eggs in their shells (which were 5/6 water anyway)

> **I remember . . . our Malcolm coming home . . . he was in the Merchant Navy and he brought three bananas . . . I ate a banana . . . and threw the banana skin down to watch people's faces . . . There was kids who didn't know what a banana was.**
>
> *Cumbrian man reminiscing, 1976*

The annual average volume of food imports in the 1930s was 22 million tons; by 1943 it was down to half that amount, thanks to advances in food technology which made it possible to send carcase meat boned and 'telescoped' and milk and eggs in dehydrated powder form.

> **RECIPE: Pork & Leek Pie**
> Wash and trim 6 medium-sized leeks and cut into 1 inch pieces. Do the same with one pound of streaky pork. Arrange layer of leeks and pork alternately in a greased pie-dish, sprinkling each layer with salt, pepper and a pinch of sage. Dissolve a tablespoonful of HP sauce in a cupful of water and pour over. Cover with a layer of potato mashed with warm milk. Bake in a moderate oven for one and a half hours. Serves 6.

NEW RECIPES

Shortages of familiar foods and the arrival of new ones meant a revolution in cooking methods. Housewives, with the enthusiastic help of the Ministry's 'Food Advice Division', learned how to make 'Woolton Pie' (a meatless concoction of root vegetables and oatmeal) and to use dried elderberries instead of currants when baking cakes.

Recipes were invented to persuade them to make marmalade out of carrots and to try to get their families eating nettles and even crows. Mysterious ingredients were disguised by even more mysterious names such as 'Commando Casserole' and 'MI5 Pudding'. Attempts to promote whalemeat were largely unsuccessful (it was just too revolting) but many people who before the war would have refused to eat offal (liver, kidneys, brains, hearts) now found it not only nutritious but tasty – if you could get it.

EATING OUT

With so many people working or living away from home mass catering took on a new importance. Before the war about 250,000 children were eating school dinners; by 1945 1,850,000 were. In 1939 there were 1,500 factory canteens, by 1945 18,500. Communal feeding centres were established for the general public. At Churchill's insistence they were renamed 'British Restaurants'. By 1945 there were 2,000 of them, serving 500,000 meals a day. From June 1942 onwards no restaurant was allowed to serve a meal costing more than five shillings (25p) – which was still five times the average charge in a British Restaurant.

THE LEGACY

Britain's wartime diet was adequate if very boring. Before 1939 there had been 350 different kinds of biscuit on sale – during the war only twenty. Thanks to rationing the diet of the poorest sections of society actually improved in the course of the war, partly because they got a better share of body-building protein foods, partly because

A restaurant whose front has been boarded-up after being bombed-out uses the free space to advertise.

they couldn't indulge their usual taste for sweets and biscuits. Evacuation meant that many inner-city children got really fresh produce for the first time in their lives.

> . . . stop and think before you sound off about . . . cold boiled potatoes . . . if you are invited into a British home and the host exhorts you to 'eat up – there's plenty on the table' go easy. It may be the family's rations for a whole week spread out to show their hospitality.
>
> *US War Department pamphlet, 1942, 'A Short Guide to Great Britain'*

The standard of diet actually fell at the end of the war when the sudden cessation of Lend-Lease trade with the USA coincided with a severe world shortage of cereals, made worse in Britain by the harsh winter of 1947.

A lasting legacy of war-time food policy has been increased consumer protection. The 1943 Defence (Sale of Food) Regulations gave the government powers to control not only what went into prepared foods but also how they were labelled and advertised. In 1955 these powers became the basis of a Food and Drugs Act and Food Hygiene Regulations to protect the public against adulterated or contaminated foods and false claims to nutritional value.

RATIONING TIMELINE

1940 January rationing begins.
Weekly rations per person:
ham-/bacon 4 ozs; sugar 12 ozs; butter 4 ozs
March meat rationed
July tea rationed 2 ozs a week

1941 March jam, marmalade & syrup rationed
May cheese rationed 1 oz per week
December points system introduced

1947 bread and potatoes rationed

1954 end of food rationing

MUSIC WHILE YOU WORK

THE BATTLE FOR PRODUCTION

Modern warfare means mass destruction which in turn requires mass production. Losses of planes, ships and equipment have to be replaced constantly for a nation even to maintain, let alone increase, its fighting strength.

The bare statistics of British wartime industrial effort show impressive expansion. Aircraft output, a mere 2,800 units in 1938, rose to 8,000 in 1939, 20,000 by 1941 and 26,000 by 1943. Tank production quadrupled between 1940 and 1942, while machine tool output tripled over the same period.

Partly this was achieved by the introduction of new technology, much of it from the United States. But the other essential factor was the increase in the labour force of the war industries, despite the losses caused by recruitment into the armed forces. This was brought about in three main ways – by absorbing the pre-war unemployed (there were still a million in 1940); by transferring (mostly female) labour out of 'non-essential' industries; and by mobilizing women who, before the war, had not worked in industry or, in many cases, had not worked at all.

The Minister of Labour could, in theory, compel women aged $18\frac{1}{2}$ to 50 into war work. In practice little compulsion was required. Although women with children

> **Nothing that a woman can do, or can learn to do, should be allowed to absorb a man of military age.**
>
> *Ernest Bevin, Minister of Labour, 1943*

> **I cannot offer them a delightful life. I want them to come forward in the spirit that they are going to suffer some inconvenience but with some determination to help us through.**
>
> *Ernest Bevin, Minister of Labour, appeals for women factory-workers, March 1941*

under fourteen were not required to work, one in seven still chose to do so and many more did part-time industrial work or voluntary service unpaid.

> ### Examples of Reserved Occupations
>
> | | | |
> |---|---|---|
> | Engineer | Fireman | Draughtsman |
> | Farmer | Bus Driver | Coalminer |
> | Policeman | Train Driver | Merchant Seaman |

Another minor but crucial factor was the return to work of retired men, many of whom were able to act as instructors of the unskilled. The need to upgrade skills was urgent and by mid-1942 the number of skilled workers in the engineering industries had doubled.

Changes in numbers of women employed 1939–43	
Distribution	− 6,000
Services	+ 58,000
Textiles	− 165,000
Clothing	− 149,000
Admin/Clerical	+ 480,000
Engineering/Aircraft/Ships	+1,197,000
Manufacturing	− 48,000
Food	− 18,000
Chemicals	+ 220,000
Agriculture	+ 102,000
Transport	+ 147,000
Other	+ 531,000

A factory girl at work.

Many new factories were established in the countryside or former 'depressed areas' to be safer from bombing and to 'mop up' local labour which might otherwise be unemployed. Scotland had both attractions for new establishments.

Arthur Marwick, Scottish historian − Britain in the Century of Total War (1968)

INGENUITY AND INVENTION

The war gave an immense stimulus to the nation's resourcefulness. An outstanding example of industrial ingenuity was the Mosquito aeroplane. As early as 1938 the de Havilland company, realizing that aluminium and alloy steels would be in short supply in a war, set their design team to produce a high-performance plane made entirely of wood. The resulting Mosquito was to serve as a precision bomber, a fighter and a photographic reconnaissance plane. With a speed of over 400 mph it was, until the arrival of jets, the fastest plane in the service of the RAF. Over 8,000 were produced, many of the parts being made in small workshops in the East End of London which before the war had been turning out cocktail cabinets and ladies dressing-tables.

Materials Salvaged for Recycling		
Rubber scraps	Kettles & saucepans	Rags
Tin cans	Toothpaste tubes	Leather
Tin baths	Bones	Paper

Far more profound in the long run, of course, was the effect of the war in promoting scientific research, which led to the development of the atomic bomb (and therefore, later, atomic power) and which turned penicillin from an interesting curiosity (discovered by accident in 1928) into a life-saving 'magic bullet' which saved an estimated 3,000 lives on D-Day alone. Other revolutionary inventions which grew out of wartime experiments include the transistor and the computer.

MORALE

In the interests of raising productivity wartime managers were keen to promote the welfare of their workers. As it could be scientifically demonstrated that providing them with a hot meal would sustain their levels of energy and alertness through long shifts, a works canteen was regarded as essential in all larger premises. Rather more surprising was the discovery that operatives engaged on repetitive mechanical tasks performed better if they were stimulated by loudspeakers playing lively music. The BBC obligingly came up with two daily half-hour doses of 'Music While You Work', skilfully timed to lift listeners through the mid-morning and mid-afternoon slumps which otherwise tended to occur. The music played was

always instrumental as early experiments showed that workers otherwise often stopped to write down the words of 'vocals'.

One very influential study of industrial morale was undertaken single-handed by a 27 year-old former employee of the social survey organization Mass Observation. For 18 months she kept a detailed diary while working as a machinist in a new factory in Wiltshire which was making top-secret aircraft components. She found to her surprise that her fellow workers had very little interest in their work or understanding of why it was important to the war effort.

The works manager blamed symptoms of low morale such as timewasting, absenteeism and 'lavatory-mongering' on the failure of official propaganda to inform and motivate machineshop women. The Mass Observation reporter came up with a far more down-to-earth explanation: that after working twelve-hour shifts for weeks on end the women had neither the time nor the energy nor the incentive to take the slightest interest in work or war.

	No. of Trade Unions	Members	Days lost in strikes
1939	1,019	6,298,000	1,360,000
1940	1,004	6,613,000	940,000
1941	996	7,165,000	1,080,000
1942	991	7,867,000	1,527,000
1943	987	8,174,000	1,808,000
1944	963	8,087,000	3,714,000
1945	781	7,875,000	2,835,000

> . . . the average working-class woman's interest in the war is kept alive, not so much by the large-scale tragedies, but by the personal inconveniences: rationing, blackout, shortages and so on. And from these inconveniences someone who works in a war factory, with an adequate canteen, for twelve hours a day, is automatically excluded. There is nothing left to keep alive in her even the slightest degree of interest . . .
>
> *Mass Observation, 1943*

It is worth noting, however, that, despite the concern over low morale absenteeism in this factory was not high and the quality of the product was satisfactory.

THE WOMEN'S WAR	
December 1939	Women arms workers demand equal pay with men
March 1941	Government calls for 100,000 women to enter factories
November 1942	Church of England ends rule requiring women to wear hats in church
May 1943	Women aged 18/45 made liable to compulsory part-time war-work
July 1943	Report shows women's pay has risen 80 per cent since 1938
March 1944	Ban on marriage of women teachers ended because of their 'great war effort'

WARTIME PAY

The pressure to encourage higher output from skilled workers in industry meant that, thanks to the payment of piece-work rates and plenty of overtime, by 1944 average earnings had risen 11 per cent higher than the cost of living since 1939. Heavily graduated income-tax, which meant that the richest paid 95 per cent in the £, depressed middle-class incomes by about 7 per cent between 1938 and 1947. Thanks to price controls, tax changes and increased employment opportunities working-class purchasing-power may have risen by as much as a quarter between 1938 and 1948.

Of course, earnings varied greatly between industries. Average weekly earnings were between £6 and £7 but a farm labourer made only about £4, though he usually had a rent-free cottage and much free food. A skilled worker in the booming aircraft industry, by contrast, could make two or even three times the national average. The pay of servicemen cannot easily be compared with that of civilians, as their living-expenses were taken care of and much of what they bought through the NAAFI (government-controlled cafe-cum-stores) was also subsidized.

Nevertheless war-time inflation eroded their pay sufficiently badly to cause widespread grumbling, furious debates in Parliament and and a number of regradings upwards.

Telephones provided the vital link between incidents and emergency services during air-raids.

LIVING ON LEFT-OVERS

With top priority going to war production there was little official concern to maintain civilian living standards beyond a bare minimum — except in the all-important question of diet. Overall it is reckoned that they fell by about 50 per cent. Shortages of steel, rubber, wood and aluminium meant that there was little to spare for the production of furniture, sports goods or kitchen utensils. Everyday essentials like razor-blades, spare parts for bicycles and teats for babies' bottles were often completely unobtainable.

A 'Utility' fur coat of 'shorn lamb', a spring mode for 1945, priced £24.

Household Items Often in Short Supply

Cutlery & crockery	Curtains & towels
Shoes, stockings, shoelaces	Pillows & blankets
Alarm Clocks	Polish, glue & candles
Safety Pins	Toys

But the decline in standards of personal comfort was most evident in the matter of clothing. American troops were warned not to be shocked: 'If British civilians look dowdy and badly dressed it is not because they do not like good clothes or know how to wear them. All clothing is rationed. Old clothes are 'good form''.

I know all the women will look smart, but we men may look shabby. If we do we must not be ashamed. In war the term 'battle-stained' is an honourable one.

President of the Board of Trade, June 1941

Men were, in effect, allowed one new suit every other year; and in the interests of economy it had to be single-breasted without cuff-buttons or trouser turn-ups. It was forbidden by law to make long trousers for boys under twelve.

Fashion-conscious women were relieved to find that many of the simplified 'Utility' dress designs were surprisingly elegant, but most sought salvation by following official exhortations to 'Make Do and Mend', using great skill and patience to recycle curtains into coats or use unrationed butter-muslin to make underwear.

THE YANKS ARE COMING!

FORTRESS OF FREEDOM

With the German conquests of 1940 Britain became the last outpost of resistance in Europe. As such it provided a base for the governments in exile of defeated countries from Estonia to the Netherlands and a refuge for a motley band of fighters from Belgian soldiers to Norwegian seamen.

The first to catch the public imagination were the foreign pilots who were numbered among 'the Few'. Of the 1500 fighter pilots who defended British air-space during the Battle of Britain almost 10 per cent were Polish. These 145 young men destroyed 219 enemy aircraft, plus a further 41 'probables' and another 40 damaged. More than a dozen won the Distinguished Flying Cross and seven the Distinguished Service Medal. Thirty-one were killed in the course of these operations. No. 303 Squadron, an entirely Polish unit, achieved the highest individual score of any squadron in the entire campaign – 125 'kills', 14 'probables' and 9 damaged. There were also other separate national contingents such as the Free French and the Czechs. One Czech ace, Josef Frantisek, had seventeen kills in a single month and scored the third highest total achieved by any single pilot.

> **It will be a splendid episode in the history of the empire if Australian, New Zealand and Canadian troops defend the Motherland against invasion**
>
> *Winston Churchill, June 1940*

In 1941 the Australians and New Zealanders went on to fight with great distinction in North Africa while the Canadians bore the brunt of the terrible losses suffered in the commando raids on the French coastal ports of Dieppe and St. Nazaire. A number of cemeteries in British towns set apart a special plot as a 'Canadian corner'.

THE YANKS ARE COMING!

Some 'Yanks' came even before the American declaration of war in December 1941. The most noticeable were the fliers of the Eagles Squadron, some of whom were experienced airline pilots, others young volunteers who had already fought in the French air force or crossed the border to join up in Canada. The first to be killed in defence of Britain, Pilot Officer William Fisk Jr, was given the single honour of a memorial in the crypt of St.

February 1941 – Corporal Heller, an American fighting with the Free French, marries a girl from Hampstead, London who was a volunteer helper at the Eagle Club, a centre for servicemen on leave.

Paul's Cathedral. By October 1941 there were three Eagles Squadrons. In September 1942 they were finally transferred to US command, taking their Spitfires with them.

> **America is sending the goods, though it is time she came in properly. It is difficult to know what is keeping them 'shivering on the brink . . .**
>
> *Clara Milburn, English housewife, 22 June 1941*

Other American volunteers had by then also served in the Royal Navy and the Canadian army. But the first American serviceman officially to set foot on British soil (in Northern Ireland) was Private First Class Milburn Henke from Minnesota who stepped ashore on Monday, 26 January 1942.

> **Be friendly – but don't intrude . . .**
> **You are higher paid than the British 'Tommy'. Don't rub it in . . .**
> **Don't show off or brag or bluster . . .**
> **Don't make fun of British speech or accents. You sound just as funny to them . . .**
> **Don't try to tell the British that America won the last war.**
> **NEVER criticize the King or Queen.**
>
> *US War Department Pamphlet, 1942 'A Short Guide to Great Britain'*

(In fact a whole battalion had already landed before the carefully staged arrival of this 'typical GI' but the press discreetly ignored this in the interests of good publicity.) By D-Day, 6 June 1944, almost two million more 'Yanks' would have followed in his footsteps.

THE FRIENDLY INVASION

Among the young the American servicemen received an eager welcome. Some, like band-leader Glenn Miller and film star James Stewart were really famous household names; but they all came with the halo of Hollywood around them and most were quite willing to indulge British fantasies by claiming to come from Texas or California or some other glamorous state, even if they actually came from New Jersey or North Dakota. They were assumed to be experts in the 'jitterbug' and other fashionable dances. They were confident, friendly and well-fed. They wore elegant, well-cut uniforms. They earned between three and seven times as much as the average British serviceman. They could afford to be generous and they were, freely giving out chewing-gum, candy bars and Camel cigarettes.

> **To go to one of their bases was absolutely fantastic because there was no shortage of anything . . . plenty of food and drink and fantastic great iced cakes . . . All the girls were doing it.**
>
> *Cambridge woman reminiscing, 1988*

American troops rarely had problems getting local girls to come to their camp dances. If they were invited back into a threadbare British home they often brought a bottle of 'Bourbon' for Dad, chocolates for Mum and real American comic books for the kid brother, as well as much-prized nylon stockings for the girlfriend herself. In the end over 60,000 British women were to become 'GI Brides'. (Many more were no doubt cruelly disappointed to find that they were not going to become brides.) A special camp had to be set up at the end of the war just to handle the outflow of newly-weds back to 'the States'.

Older people were more guarded in their response. Many of them, perhaps, thought of America not as the home of 'swing' music and movie stars but as the home of gangsters and corrupt politicians. Some found American troops loud-mouthed and wasteful with precious food and supplies.

> **They do not walk or march smartly like our men . . . No crisp tramp-tramp, but just managing to keep fairly in step.**
>
> *Clara Milburn, English housewife, 30 March 1944*

Whatever impression they actually made it would be wrong to accuse the Americans of not trying very hard indeed to mind their manners and take note of British customs and attitudes.

> **There must be many older women like myself who have to do more travelling than they would choose these days, and if it were not for the unfailing courtesy of all ranks of the United States services in offering us their seats, the journeys often would be more arduous than they are.**
>
> *Letter to* The Times, *September 1943*

Apart from briefing troops by means of pamphlets and lectures the US War Department also commissioned a film, 'Welcome to Britain', in which actor Burgess Meredith, playing the role of a GI, warns fellow Americans not to laugh at Scots in kilts etc. One American 'custom', however, caused more difficulty than any other — racism.

Show me that again — US pilot teaching how to 'jitterbug'.

TWO KINDS OF AMERICAN

American troops were divided into white and 'coloured' units, the latter being usually assigned to cooking, driving and other such support services rather than to combat. Out-

Hi there! American troops make friends with local children in Northern Ireland, 1942.

side the major ports like London and Liverpool few British people had ever seen a black person, except on the cinema screen, dancing and playing jazz. When British girls began to dance with black GIs the outcome could often be vicious brawls between black and white Americans.

> . . . occasional cases will occur which might arouse the resentment and even anger of British troops and civilians who witness them . . . it is obviously highly unsuitable to try to interfere in these instances . . . attempts to break down the various forms of social regulation accepted by the average American family, white or coloured, is not likely to achieve any good purpose but on the contrary might well lead to trouble and even violence, especially where women are concerned.
>
> *Journal of US Army Bureau of Current Affairs, 1941*

In general 'trouble' was avoided by working out a sort of informal apartheid system which allowed white and black troops out of camp and 'on the town' on separate nights.

IN MEMORIAM

Some idea of the closeness of Anglo-American relations can be gauged by the depth of British reaction to the death of President Roosevelt in April 1945. Clara Milburn noted the event in her diary as 'tragic news', 'a great loss to everyone.' After the war a public appeal was launched to collect money for a statue to his memory. No one was allowed to give more than five shillings (25p). The £10,000 needed was raised in twenty-four hours.

It took rather longer to raise the much larger sum needed to reconstruct the bombed-out Jesus Chapel behind the High Altar of St. Paul's Cathedral as the 'American Memorial Chapel' with stained-glass windows bearing the arms of the (then) forty-eight states of America. But the bulk of the money needed also came from the donations of ordinary people, much of it collected by passing a bucket round at cinemas. At the dedication of the chapel General Eisenhower, ex-Supreme Allied Commander, presented a 'Book of Honor' containing the names of 28,000 US servicemen who died on active duty while based in the United Kingdom. Many lie buried in the beautiful American Memorial Cemetery at Madingley, outside Cambridge.

KEEP SMILING THROUGH

OUT OF PRINT

War has been defined as short periods of terror divided by long periods of boredom. One by-product of this in wartime Britain was that many people began to read 'serious' books for the first time in their lives. At first the motive might be to while away the time stuck on a railway station waiting for a train that wasn't running or to kill an evening in a gun emplacement miles from the nearest pub. Later it might be the wish to read 'the book of the film' (like 'Gone with the Wind') or even, as people begin to think about the post-war world, to learn more about politics.

> **People are reading more and reading good stuff. It is as if the war has brought home to us all the seriousness of existence. We want to find out more about the universe while we can.**
>
> *T. S. Eliot, poet, BBC broadcast, December 1941*

The BBC's radio serialization of 'War and Peace', as an indirect tribute to our Soviet allies, made this three volume classic the foreign bestseller of the war. (The outright bestseller, however, was the HMSO pamphlet on 'The Battle of Britain', which sold five million copies). Gardening books also sold well, thanks to the 'Dig for Victory' campaign.

Publishers struggled against the odds to carry on their business. The great London raid of 29 December 1940 destroyed some 5 million books stored in the area around St. Paul's. It was estimated that to keep bringing out new titles the trade would need just over 1 per cent of national paper consumption; it was allocated less than half of that and so the annual number of new titles published fell from 15,000 in 1939 to 6,700 in 1943. Whole categories of books — dictionaries, nursing texts and the soothing novels of Jane Austen — became so scarce that they were often sold 'under the counter' to favoured customers only.

A GOOD NIGHT OUT

At the very beginning of the war the government ordered the closure of cinemas and theatres, fearful of the effects of a bomb on such vulnerable and concentrated targets. Later on, having worked out that an audience of 1,500 packed into a cinema on a cold winter evening uses far less fuel than if they were all in their separate homes, officialdom reversed its attitude and positively encouraged people to go to the movies. (Bombs did

'If the war didn't kill you, it was bound to start you thinking.' George Orwell 1941.

indeed sometimes make direct hits on cinemas and theatres, inflicting heavy casualties.)

> **May I be allowed to protest vehemently against the order to close all theatres and picture-houses during the war? It seems to me a masterstroke of unimaginative stupidity. During the last war we had 80,000 soldiers on leave to amuse every night ... We have hundreds of thousands of evacuated children to be kept out of mischief ... All actors, variety-artists, musicians and entertainers ... should be exempted from every form of service except their own all-important professional one.**
>
> *George Bernard Shaw, Letter to* The Times
> *4 September 1939*

> **For teenagers it was heaven ... I had brothers away fighting; naturally I worried about them, but we were having such a good time that you didn't realize that they were away actually fighting in the war ... I would go to a dance every night if there was one.**
>
> *Cumbrian woman reminiscing, 1976*

British cinema audiences soon found to their surprise that they were watching not American but British movies and, even more to their surprise, liking them. American westerns, thrillers and musicals still offered first-class escapism but Hollywood's attempts to portray the war scene that the British knew at first hand seemed as inept as they were well-intentioned. Building on a tradition of documentary film-making which was the great native strength of pre-war British cinema, film-makers began to shoot subjects whose realism audiences could accept and appreciate.

Noel Coward, multi-talented star of the 1930s stage, set the trend with 'In Which We Serve', based on the exploits and sinking of HMS *Kelly*, the destroyer commanded by his friend Lord Louis Mountbatten. Although professional actors (John Mills, Bernard Miles) took the leading roles most of the crew were played by serving sailors on shore

ENSA concert on an improvised stage in a factory, October 1941.

leave after being torpedoed. At first the Ministry of Information tried to ban the film because it showed a British ship sinking. The personal intervention of the King secured its release – to triumphant success. Over three hundred other feature-length British films were produced during the course of the war, portraying not only the efforts of the fighting services ('Desert Victory', 'Target for Tonight', 'One of our Aircraft is Missing') but also of the merchant navy (San Demetrio, London) and the munitions girls ('Millions Like Us').

A different level of inspiration came from young Laurence Olivier's flamboyant production of Shakespeare's 'Henry V'. Made in neutral Ireland, it was released on the eve of the D-day invasion – with the original scenes about English traitors cut from the script.

There were also hundreds more short documentaries carrying 'public service' messages about health, nutrition and the real possibility that one could after all enjoy a bath with only the regulation five inches of water. That said, the most popular film of the entire war was still the Hollywood blockbuster 'Gone with the Wind' which ran for four years non-stop in London.

Live theatre also kept going and the chaos of the times helped many new talents to emerge, as did the sponsorship of CEMA (Council for the Encouragement of Music and the Arts), the forerunner of the post-war Arts Council. The lunchtime classical concerts of Dame Myra Hess in the sandbagged National Gallery and the ethereal performances of ballerina Margot Fonteyn in parks and aircraft hangars really did bring 'culture to the masses' – or at least a few of them.

Servicemen on leave in London, however, tended to make for the Windmill Theatre which offered a day and night burlesque programme of scantily-clad show-girls and stand-up comedians. Serious interest in the opposite sex, however, invariably entailed a visit to the Lyceum Ballroom or Hammersmith Palais, as dancing remained by far the most popular of all popular entertainments.

A GOOD NIGHT IN

The dangers of the blackout and blitz, the difficulties of transport, the demands of family and 'fire-watching', and the fact of sheer exhaustion meant that most people spent far more nights in than out.

> **The village has come to life again, since it has become so difficult to get to our nearest town, six miles away . . . we have whist drives . . . they are really like a big family gathering . . . And . . . there are auctions, jumble sales and teas in aid of this and that . . . we really know and enjoy our community as we did not, when transport was easier.**
>
> *Oxfordshire villager quoted in Farmers Weekly, October 1944*

Radio was Britain's vital supplier of 'information, education and entertainment'. Listening to the 9 o'clock news became a national ritual and made household names of newsreaders Bruce Belfrage and John Snagge and of front-line reporters Richard Dimbleby and Wynford Vaughan-Thomas.

> **Each evening at 9, everyone stops . . . for the evening news. It is almost an offence to telephone at the hour of the BBC bulletins and as you walk along the pavements the announcer's voice echoes through all open windows.**
>
> *Cecil Beaton, professional photographer, September 1944*

Jump to it! Gunners, rehearsing for a Christmas pantomime, have no time to change before going into action.

The most consistently popular programmes, however, were comedy shows such as 'Band Waggon' and 'ITMA' (It's That Man Again), which starred Tommy Handley, who couldn't sing and could scarcely be said to act. His sudden death in 1944 stunned the nation. ITMA's peculiar humour exploited the ability of radio to dispense with and yet go beyond the scenery, costume, make-up and narrative logic required by visual drama; it rested on catchphrases which passed into everyday speech ('After you, Claude'; 'I don't mind if I do'; and 'Can I do you now, Sir?') and mythical characters everyone could imagine as they wished (Mrs. Mopp; Colonel Chinstrap; Mona Lott).

Other popular programmes were the 'Radio Doctor' ('How are your bowels?'); the 'Brains Trust' ('It all depends what you mean by . . .'); and the 'Postscript' talks of plain-spoken Yorkshire playwright J. B. Priestley. Churchill's occasional set-piece addresses to the nation, however, topped them all.

WAR GAMES

Professionally-organized sport was brought to a crashing halt by the outbreak of hostilities and the consequent official ban on the public assembly of large crowds. First-class cricket was suspended for the duration and footballers were summarily sacked. Brentford and QPR players went off and joined the

Radio star Tommy Handley in an unusual role — on the cinema screen.

police. A large number of professional sports-men served out their time as physical training instructors in the services.

> **Lord Leconfield, hunting in the winter of 1940 . . . rode towards . . . a village football match. He stood up in his stirrups and shouted 'Haven't you people got anything better to do in wartime than to play football?'**
>
> *Quoted in Raymond Carr — English Fox Hunting*

Petrol shortages, the requisitioning of arenas and the impossibility of artificial lighting during blackouts wiped out speedway, compe-titive tennis, ice-hockey and evening grey-hound racing. On the other hand, empty roads made cycling a pleasure.

Sport was, however, too central a part of the way of life of a nation which saw itself as above all 'sporting' for it to be totally sup-pressed or abandoned. Through improvisation a new pattern of fixtures emerged. Cricketers took up the one-day match. Ex-professional footballers played in regional leagues, wearing the colours of the side nearest to where they were working or stationed. Rugby Union players played Rugby League.

The authorities came to understand that sport, far from being a useless distraction, could positively assist the war effort by raising standards of fitness and public morale and that specially staged events could raise large sums

Killing time. ARP crews while away off-duty hours.

for war charities. Such events included exhibitions of tennis, golf and boxing as well as soccer and cricket matches. In 1943 the Duke of Gloucester, patron of the joint charity supporting the Red Cross and St. John's Ambulance, announced that sporting events had so far contributed more than a million pounds to their funds.

The continuance of horse racing was much criticized on the grounds that it did nothing to contribute to anyone's fitness except the horses, raised nothing for charity and was a total waste of the time, money and petrol of the racegoers who attended meetings. Nevertheless horse racing continued much as before, with the Derby, unlike the unofficial FA Cup Finals, retaining its full pre-war status. Perhaps the fact that the King and Queen were keen owners and spectators was not entirely irrelevant. In 1942 His Majesty managed to combine duty with pleasure by making a lightning agricultural tour of Cambridgeshire before going on to Newmarket to watch his horse, Sun Chariot, win the Oaks.

NEW JERUSALEM?

LOOKING FORWARD TO VICTORY

By the end of 1941, with the US and USSR as well as the UK at war with Nazi Germany most British people felt, like Churchill, that the eventual victory of the 'Grand Alliance' was certain. It would take years but, given the huge resources of American industry and the immense manpower of the Soviet forces, Germany would be crushed in the end.

Many remembered the First World War and the vague idealism of its war aims – to rescue 'gallant little Belgium', to 'make the world safe for democracy' and even to fight the war because it would be 'the war to end all wars'. The end when it came had come suddenly. There had been no detailed planning ahead for a 'post-war world' – only Prime Minister Lloyd George's splendid slogan of 'a land fit for heroes to live in' and a general assumption that Britain could easily slip back into its old position as the focus of world trade. Instead Britain had found itself facing fierce new competition overseas, while at home the returning heroes got used to a land of strikes, slums and slump.

WAR AIMS

The men and women who fought in the Second World War wanted – demanded – something better. Far fewer saw the war as a great crusade, though fewer still were in any doubt that they were fighting against a vile and evil regime.

> We have to provide full employment: we have to rebuild Britain . . . we have to organize social services at a level which secures adequate health, nutrition and care in old age for all citizens; and we have to provide educational opportunities for all . . .
>
> *Labour Party – The Old World and the New Society, 1942*

Instead they saw the struggle as a tough and dirty job that just had to be done, a test of endurance to be endured. They might, indeed, have been willing, in the case of invasion, to fulfill Churchill's stirring prediction that they would fight on the beaches, in the streets and in the hills and 'never surrender'. But that did not mean that they were fighting to defend the Britain of the 1930s – the Britain of hunger marches and hopelessness.

VE (Victory in Europe) Day in London – 8 May 1945.

Churchill, although famously assured of victory, was wary of discussing war aims in more specific terms. Knowing how desperate Britain's position was when he took office he defined the national objective in the simplest possible terms – 'to survive'. Even when the strategic position was transformed by Britain's alliance with the US and USSR he tried to discourage discussion of post-war conditions. He believed that the British people would make whatever sacrifices they were called upon for in order to win victory – but that they would never forgive a government that raised impossible hopes or made false promises. Knowing that the war would exhaust the British economy and be followed by years more of shortages, Churchill believed it both wrong and foolish to allow people to think that victory could immediately guarantee a Britain free of problems and poverty.

POST-WAR PROMISES

December 1942	School meals to be made permanent
April 1943	First plans announced for a 'national health service'
July 1943	London plans a ring road round the capital
February 1944	BBC pledges a schools radio service
March 1944	Government sets post-war house-building target of 300,000 a year
April 1944	BBC pledges to provide a TV service for all

A precious passport – the civilian ration book.

THE BEVERIDGE REPORT

The mood of a people at war was not, however, something even Churchill could command. And that mood was revealed by the enthusiastic reaction to the publication of the 'Beveridge Report' at the end of 1942. Sir William Beveridge was a former civil servant who had helped Churchill, then President of the Board of Trade, introduce Britain's first scheme of 'National Insurance' in 1911.

> **Organization of social insurance should be treated as one part only of a comprehensive policy of social progress. Social insurance . . . is an attack upon Want. But Want is only one of five giants of the road of reconstruction and in some ways the easiest to attack. The others are Disease, Ignorance, Squalor and Idleness.**
>
> *Beveridge Report, 1942*

In the years between the wars the provision of benefits covering unemployment, sickness and other such difficulties had grown into a chaotic mass of overlapping schemes and confusing rules. Beveridge was therefore appointed to head a committee which would recommend how the situation could be reorganized and tidied up after the war. His 'Report,' however, went far beyond his basic brief and set out a vision of a comprehensive system of social security, medical support and expanded opportunity in employment, education and housing.

> **Too much has been made of the Beveridge Report. It is no revolutionary document. Mainly it is a co-ordination of existing services with certain modest additions . . . It is a beginning, not an end . . .**
>
> *Daily Mirror, 16 February 1943*

HOPES AND FEARS

Available in both a full and summary form, the 'Beveridge Report' sold 635,000 copies. It was followed by other measures which either pledged new policies for the post-war era or actually enshrined them in law. In February 1943 a Ministry of Town and Country Planning was established; under the influence of Professor Patrick Abercrombie of University College, London plans were drawn up to build a ring of 'New Towns' thirty miles or more from London where ex-slumdwellers could begin a new life in new surroundings.

> **We don't go back on all we said when the country was in danger . . . Instead of guessing and grabbing, we plan. Instead of competing, we co-operate.**
>
> *Ex-serviceman in J. B. Priestley's novel – Three Men in New Suits (1945)*

In November 1943 Lord Woolton, the successful Minister of Food, was appointed Minister of Reconstruction, with a seat in the War Cabinet. An Education Act, promoted by R. A. Butler in 1944, proposed to give free secondary education for all and to raise the school-leaving age to fifteen and then sixteen. In the same year a 'White Paper' (i.e. a statement of intent rather than an actual law) committed post-war governments to follow policies which would lead to full employment and another sketched out plans for a comprehensive national health service.

> **This was a people's war. Not only were their needs considered. They themselves wanted to win . . . Imperial greatness was on the way out; the welfare state was on the way in. The British empire declined; the condition of the people improved.**
>
> *A. J. P. Taylor, English historian – English History 1914–1945 (1965)*

Even as the war ended it seemed that Churchill had been proved right. On August 14, the day Japan surrendered, the Treasury warned the newly-elected Labour government that Britain was facing 'an economic Dunkirk' and was '. . . virtually bankrupt . . . the economic basis for the hopes of the public non-existent'. Fighting the war had cost Britain 400,000 lives and massive foreign debts. The merchant fleet was 30 per cent smaller than it had been in 1939 and exports were down by more than 50 per cent. But the war had given an immense boost to science and the modern industries which depended on science – electrical goods, vehicles, chemicals and machine tools. With a new industrial base the British people could, with difficulty, go forward. And they did.

FURTHER READING

GENERAL SURVEYS

Ronald Blythe (ed) *Components of the Scene: An Anthology of the Prose and Poetry of the Second World War*, Penguin, 1966

Susan Briggs *Keep Smiling Through: The Home Front 1939–45*, Weidenfeld & Nicolson, 1975

Angus Calder *The People's War*, Cape, 1969

Paul Fussell *Wartime: Understanding and Behaviour in the Second World War*, Oxford UP, 1989

Robert Kee & Joanna Smith *We'll Meet Again: Photographs of Daily Life in Britain During World War II*, Dent, 1984

Peter Lewis *A People's War*, Methuen, 1986

Norman Longmate *How We Lived Then*, Hutchinson, 1971

Arthur Marwick *The Home Front*, Thames & Hudson, 1976

Rayne Minns *Bombers & Mash: The Domestic Front 1939–45*, Virago, 1980

Leonard Mosley *Backs to the Wall: London Under Fire 1940–45*, Weidenfeld & Nicolson, 1971

Henry Pelling *Britain and the Second World War*, Collins, 1970

Godfrey Smith *How It Was in the War*, Pavilion, 1989

SPECIAL ASPECTS

John Costello *Love, Sex and War: Changing Values 1939–45*, Collins, 1985

Juliet Gardiner *Over Here? The GIs in Wartime Britain*, Collins & Brown, 1992

Peter & Leni Gillman *Collar the Lot! How Britain Interned and Expelled its Wartime Refugees*, Quartet, 1980

Charles Graves *London Transport at War*, Oldcastle Books, 1989

Tom Harrisson *Living Through the Blitz*, Penguin, 1990

Robert Hewison *Under Siege: Literary life in London 1939–45*, Weidenfeld & Nicolson, 1978

Tom Hopkinson *Picture Post 1938–50*, Penguin, 1970

Geoff Hurd (ed.) *National Fictions: World War Two in British Films and Television*, BFI Books, 1984

Carlton Jackson *Who Will Take Our Children? The Story of the Evacuation in Britain*, Methuen, 1985

Mass Observation *War Factory*, Cresset Press, 1987

Jane Waller & Michael Vaughan-Rees *Blitz: The Civilian War 1940–45*, Macdonald Optima, 1990

Robert Westall *Children of the Blitz: Memories of Wartime Childhood*, Viking, 1985

David Wicks *The Day They Took the Children*, Bloomsbury, 1989

Marion Yass *This is Your War: Home Front Propaganda in the Second World War*, HMSO, 1983

DIARIES AND MEMOIRS

Margery Allingham *The Oaken Heart: The Story of an English Village at War*, Sarsen Publications, 1987

George Beardmore *Civilians at War: Journals 1938-1946*, Oxford UP, 1986

Edward Blishen *A Cack-Handed War*, Hamish Hamilton, 1983

Vera Brittain *England's Hour. An Autobiography 1939–41*, Futura, 1981

Richard Broad & Suzie Fleming (eds) *Nella Last's War: A Mother's Diary 1939–1945*, Falling Wall Press, 1981

Jonathan Croall (ed) *Don't You Know There's a War On?: The People's Voice 1939–45*, Hutchinson, 1988

Peter Donnelly *Mrs Milburn's Diaries: An Englishwoman's Day-to-Day Reflections 1939–45*, Harrap, 1979

Pete Grafton *You, You and You! The People Out of Step with World War Two*, Pluto Press, 1981

Charles Hannam *Almost an Englishman*, Andre Deutsch, 1979

Patrick Mayhew (ed.) *One Family's War*, Hutchinson, 1985

Nigel Nicolson (ed.) *Harold Nicolson: Diaries and Letters 1939–45*, Collins, 1967

FOR YOUNGER READERS

Nance Lui Fyson *Portrait of a Decade: The 1940s*, Batsford, 1988

Nance Lui Fyson *Growing Up in the Second World War*, Batsford, 1981

Sheila Gordon *A Day that Made History: 3rd September 1939*, Batsford, 1988

Maureen Hill *Growing Up at War*, Armada, 1989

C. A. R. Hills *Living Through History: The Second World War*, Batsford, 1985

Michael Rawcliffe *How It Was: Britain at War 1939–45*, Batsford, 1992

Fiona Reynoldson *The Blitz*, Wayland

Fiona Reynoldson *Evacuation*, Wayland

Fiona Reynoldson *Rationing*, Wayland

Fiona Reynoldson *Women's War*, Wayland

Stewart Ross *The Home Front*, Wayland

Stewart Ross *A Family in World War II*, Wayland, 1985

Neil Thomson *When I Was Young: World War II*, Watts

R. J. Unstead & Tim Wood *The 1940s*, Watts

INDEX